A PRIMARY SOURCE
LIBRARY OF
AMERICAN CITIZENSHIP ™

Congress

Bernadette Brexel

rosen central
Primary Source ™

The Rosen Publishing Group, Inc., New York

To Richard and Elaine

Published in 2004 by The Rosen Publishing Group, Inc.
29 East 21st Street, New York, NY 10010

Copyright © 2004 by The Rosen Publishing Group, Inc.

First Edition

Library of Congress Cataloging-in-Publication Data

Brexel, Bernadette.
Congress/by Bernadette Brexel.—1st ed.
    v. cm.—(A primary source library of American citizenship)
Includes bibliographical references and index.
Contents: Government and Congress—The Senate and the House—Capitol Hill—Duties of Congress—Congress and laws.
ISBN 0-8239-4470-0 (library binding)
1. United States. Congress—Juvenile literature. [1. United States. Congress.]
I. Title. II. Series.
JK1025.C44 2004
328.73–dc21

                                                                                    2003007579

Manufactured in the United States of America

On the cover: (top, right) drawing by P. F. Rothermel, engraved by R. Whitechurch, of the United States Senate, 1850; (background) Seventeenth Amendment to the U.S. Constitution: direct election of U.S. Senators (1913); (bottom left) President George W. Bush addressing a joint session of Congress in 2003.

Photo credits: cover, pp. 5, 8, 13 (top and bottom), 15 (top), 19, 21, 24 © AP/Wide World Photos; pp. 6, 16, 20 © Library of Congress, Prints and Photographs Division; p. 7 © Record Group II, general records of the United States government, Old Military and Civil Records, National Archives and Records Administration; p. 9 © Mark Muench/Corbis; p. 11 (top) © Mark Reinstein/Image Stock Imagery, Inc.; p. 11 (bottom) © Ellis Richard/Corbis Sygma; p. 15 (bottom) © Don Young.com; p. 17 © Architect of the Capitol; p. 18 © Annie Griffiths Belt/Corbis; pp. 22, 27, 30 © Bettmann/Corbis; p. 23 © AFP/Corbis; p. 25 © Visser Robert/Corbis Sygma; p. 28 © David J. and Janice L. Frent Collection/Corbis; p. 29 © Wally McNamee/Corbis.

Designer: Tahara Hasan; Editor: Charles Hofer; Photo Researcher: Peter Tomlinson

Contents

1 Government and Congress

Congress is an important part of the United States government. The government serves its citizens. The government protects the American people at home and throughout the world.

The government does a lot for the country. Many schools, hospitals, and parks are controlled or built by the government. The government also supports police and other public services.

Two Parts of Government

Our government is a federal government. It spreads all duties between two parts. One part is national. National government deals with matters about the whole country. The other part is made of all the state governments. State governments handle matters within each state.

Congress plays a major role in the United States government. Members of Congress must work together to better serve the American people. Here, several members of Congress break ground for the new U.S. Capitol Visitor Center in Washington, D.C.

Congress began in 1789. Congress is based on the United States Constitution. This important document was written by America's first leaders. The Constitution lists the basic laws, or rules, that our government must follow. It was written so that no one person would have too much power. Power is spread among all members in Congress.

In this engraving, President George Washington gives a speech at the 1787 Constitutional Convention in Philadelphia. The leaders who attended the convention are sometimes called the Founding Fathers of the United States.

The United States Constitution was written during the Constitutional Convention of 1787. The Constitution defines the powers of the United States government.

Congress is the part of government that makes laws. Laws control the nation and protect its people.

People who work in Congress represent the American public. They speak for the people who voted for them. They tell Congress about the needs of the people from their home state.

It is important for members of Congress to meet with the people they represent. Here, Representative Rick Renzi of Arizona meets with members of the Navajo Nation.

Congress meets in the Capitol building. It is located in Washington, D.C., on Capitol Hill. The Capitol houses both the Senate and the House of Representatives.

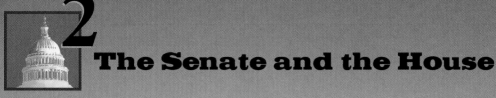

2 The Senate and the House

Congress is made of two parts, called chambers. These chambers are the Senate and the House of Representatives. The House of Representatives is also called the House. Power between the House and Senate is the same. Each can make, change, or get rid of laws.

Who's Who?

People who work in the Senate are called senators. People who work in the House are called representatives.

Members of both the Senate and the House of Representatives gather to discuss important issues. There are 435 members in the House of Representatives *(pictured above)*. The Senate *(pictured below)* has 100 members.

There are 100 members of the Senate. Each state sends two representatives to the Senate. Senators serve for six years. Senators know the needs of the voters from their state. A senator can make laws to help the people in his or her home state. Senators also try to make laws that help the nation.

Becoming a Senator

Anybody can be a senator as long as he or she
- is at least 30 years old
- has been a United States citizen for at least nine years
- is a resident of the state that he or she hopes to represent

While running for Congress, candidates must give speeches to tell the people why they would make a good senator or representative. Above, representative Richard Nixon speaks to a crowd in California in 1950. Below, Senate candidate Ron Kirk speaks to a group of supporters in Dallas, Texas, in 2002.

House representatives serve a two-year term. There are 435 members in the House. Each state has at least one representative. Some states get to have more than one representative. This is based on how many people live in that state. In 2002, California sent 53 representatives to the House. Connecticut sent 5. Alaska sent 1.

Becoming a Representative

Anybody can be a representative in the House as long as he or she

- is at least 25 years old
- has been a United States citizen for at least seven years
- is a resident of the state that he or she hopes to represent

Representative Cynthia McKinney *(above, left)* waves to supporters during her 1996 campaign. That year, McKinney was one of eleven people from Georgia elected to the House of Representatives. Don Young, pictured below, has served sixteen terms as the only member of the House representing Alaska.

Capitol Hill

The Senate and the House meet in a building in Washington, D.C., called the Capitol. The Capitol is on Capitol Hill, or "the Hill." Congress has been meeting in the Capitol since 1800. The Senate and House meet in different rooms in the Capitol. The rooms are called chambers. A meeting of the Senate or the House is called a session.

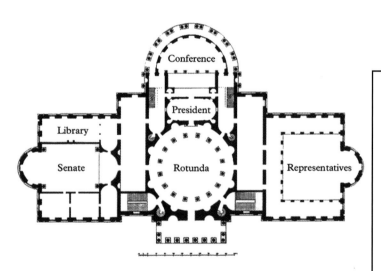

This picture shows the layout of the Capitol building. The House, Senate, and president have their own chambers. Ceremonies and special meetings are held in the Rotunda.

This photograph shows Capitol Hill. The Capitol building is in the center. Several other important government buildings surround the Capitol.

Members of Congress are not in session all the time. They are too busy. They can see what is happening in session by watching televisions in their offices. Members have offices near the Capitol. They also have offices in their home states. Members visit their home states to talk to the voters.

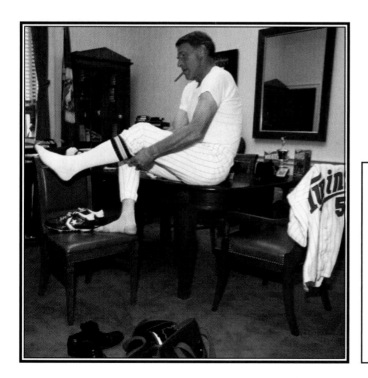

Members of Congress do have fun, too. Here, Representative Martin Sabo of Minnesota, dresses for the annual Congressional Baseball Game in 1990.

It is very important for members of Congress to stay in touch with people from their home states. Here, Representative Tom Sawyer meets with townspeople in Youngstown, Ohio.

4 Duties of Congress

Members of the Senate and the House must choose two floor leaders. Floor leaders help control what happens in the Senate and House. They are also known as majority or minority leaders. Other senators and representatives are chosen to serve as assistants to the floor leaders. They are called whips. Whips help members of Congress stay informed about important issues.

Sometimes, the floor of Congress can host debates or arguments. This drawing was done in 1850. It shows Congressman Henry Clay giving a speech on the floor of the Senate.

Members of Congress must work together to better serve the American people. Here, Senate Majority Leader Bill Frist *(center)* shakes hands with Senator Pete V. Domenici. Former Senate Majority Leader Howard Baker is pictured on the left.

The Senate and the House have special groups. These groups are called committees. Each committee takes care of an important subject like farming or energy. Committee members study the subject and try to make laws about it. The Senate has 21 committees. The House has 20. Many senators and representatives serve on more than one committee.

In the 1950s, Senator Joseph McCarthy upset many Americans with his House Un-American Activities Committee (HUAC). McCarthy used this committee to accuse people of being enemies of the American government.

Committees are formed to focus on specific issues. Committees bring several members of Congress together to address problems or issues that concern the public. Here, a committee discusses the space shuttle *Columbia* disaster in February 2003.

5 Congress and Laws

Congress makes our laws. A new law begins as a bill in either the Senate or the House. A member suggests a bill to a committee. The committee will decide to pass it or not. If the bill passes the committee, the rest of the chamber will vote on it.

YEA 90 NAY 9

H.R. 5005, the Department of Homeland Security Act

Congress made several changes to the United States government following the terrorist attacks on September 11, 2001. Here, Congress gathers to vote on creating the Homeland Security Department. Ninety votes were for creating the department, while only nine votes were against it.

The Speaker of the House acts as the leader of the House while it is in session. Newt Gingrich, pictured, was Speaker of the House from 1995 to 1999.

When the bill is passed, it is sent to the other chamber (either the Senate or the House). The other chamber must also pass the bill. The bill can then be dropped or sent back for changes. If it passes the other chamber, it is sent to the president. If the president signs it, the bill becomes a law.

Veto Power

The president can return a bill to Congress. This is called a veto. The president has ten days to decide on a bill. If the president doesn't decide in time, the bill may become a law. It will become a law if Congress was in session during the ten days.

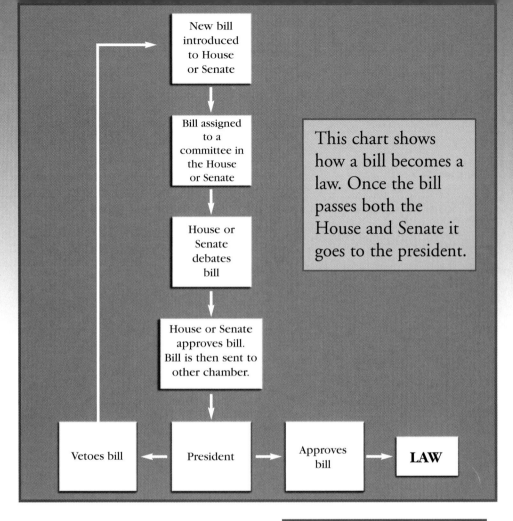

New bill introduced to House or Senate

Bill assigned to a committee in the House or Senate

House or Senate debates bill

House or Senate approves bill. Bill is then sent to other chamber.

Vetoes bill ← President → Approves bill → **LAW**

This chart shows how a bill becomes a law. Once the bill passes both the House and Senate it goes to the president.

President Lyndon B. Johnson *(pictured right)* signs the 1965 Voting Rights Bill. The new law would make it easier for African Americans and other minorities to vote.

The House suggests laws for taxes and spending. These laws decide how the government will spend its money. This money could be spent on schools, roads, hospitals, and other public services. The House can also start cases against government leaders. The leaders can be charged with breaking the law. This is called impeachment.

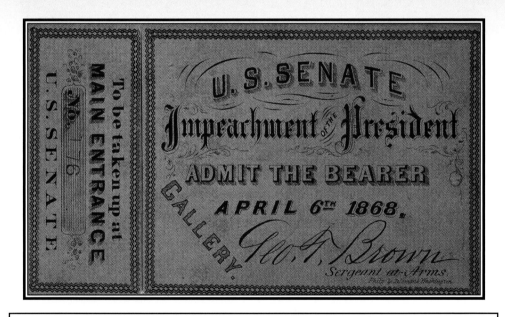

Since 1776, only two presidents have been impeached. Tickets were actually sold to attend the impeachment hearings of Andrew Johnson in 1868.

In 1998, President Bill Clinton was impeached for lying to the American public. Here he gives videotaped testimony for his trial.

The president chooses people for some important government jobs. The Senate then decides if these people actually get the jobs. The president may make treaties with other countries. A treaty is an agreement. The Senate decides on whether to make a treaty legal. The Senate also decides if an impeached leader is innocent or guilty.

In 1978, President Jimmy Carter *(center)* brought together two rivals, president Anwar Sadat of Egypt *(left)* and Israeli prime minister Menachem Begin. The three are signing an agreement to begin peace talks.

Glossary

bill (BIL) A written plan for a new law.

Capitol (KA-pih-tuhl) The building in which the national government is based. Located in Washington, D.C.

chamber (CHAYM-buhr) A large room where the Senate or the House meets.

Congress (KON-gres) The government body of the United States that makes laws. It is made up of the Senate and the House of Representatives.

Constitution (kon-stih-TOO-shun) The written document that the United States government is based upon. It went into effect in 1789.

floor leader (FLOR LEE-duhr) A member of Congress who helps control what happens during the session.

government (GUH-vern-mihnt) The system that controls a country. The people who rule or govern a country.

impeachment (im-PEECH-mihnt) The act of bringing charges against a government leader who may have done something wrong while in office.

representative (reh-prih-ZEN-tuh-tiv) Someone who is chosen to speak or act for others. Also, someone who is a member of the House of Representatives.

senator (SEH-nuh-ter) Someone who serves in the Senate.

session (SEH-shun) A series of meetings.

veto (VEE-toh) To stop a bill from becoming law.

Web Sites

Due to the changing nature of Internet links, the Rosen Publishing Group, Inc., has developed an online list of Web sites related to the subject of this book. This site is updated regularly. Please use this link to access the list:

http://www.rosenlinks.com/pslac/cong

Primary Source Image List

Page 5: Photo taken by AP photographer Dennis Cook on June 20, 2000, of several members of Congress breaking ground for the U.S. Capitol Visitor Center in Washington, D.C.

Page 6: Engraving, entitled *Convention at Philadelphia, 1787*, done in 1823 of George Washington addressing members of the Constitutional Convention. Published by Huntington & Hopkins.

Page 7: The United States Constitution. Drafted in 1787 and housed in the National Archives.

Page 8: Photo of Congressman Rick Renzi speaking with members of the Navajo Nation, April 22, 2003, by AP photographer Douglas Tesner.

Page 9: Photo of the Capitol building in Washington, D.C. Photographed by Marc Muench, ca. 1990–1995.

Page 13 (top): AP staff photo of Richard Nixon on the campaign trail, April 22, 1950.

Page 13 (bottom): Photo by AP photographer Tony Gutierrez of Senate candidate Ron Kirk, October 29, 2002.

Page 15 (top): Photo by AP photographer Ric Feld of Cynthia McKinney in Decatur, Georgia, November 5, 1996.
Page 18: Photo by Annie Griffiths Belt of Congressman Martin Sabo in Washington, D.C., July 1990.
Page 19: Photo by AP photographer Tony Dejak of Congressman Tom Sawyer speaking with supporters, May 7, 2002, in Youngstown, Ohio.
Page 20: *The United States Senate*, drawn by P. F. Rothermel, engraved by R. Whitechurch, circa 1855.
Page 21: AP photo by Susan Walsh, January 7, 2003. Pictured *(left to right)*, Howard Baker, Bill Frist, and Pete Domenici in Washington, D.C.
Page 22: Photo of Senator Joseph McCarthy in Washington, D.C., May 1954.
Page 23: Photo by Mike Theiler of joint House-Senate Appropriations Committee for a briefing on the space shuttle *Columbia* disaster, February 3, 2003, in Washington, D.C.
Page 24: Image from video by AP/CSPAN via APTN showing Senate voting results for creating the Department of Homeland Security, November 19, 2002.
Page 25: Photo by Robert Visser for Corbis Sygma of Newt Gingrich in Washington, D.C., January 4, 1995.
Page 27: Photo of President Lyndon Johnson signing Voting Rights Bill, Washington, D.C., August 6, 1965.
Page 28: Photo of Andrew Johnson impeachment ticket by David J. Frent from the David J. & Janice L. Frent Collection/CORBIS.
Page 29: Photo of video image by Wally McNamee, Washington, D.C., ca. November–December 1998.
Page 30: Photo taken September 16, 1978, in Washington, D.C.

Index

About the Author

Bernadette Brexel is a journalist and author with an avid interest in political science.

DATE DUE

MAY 2 0 2009			

FOLLETT